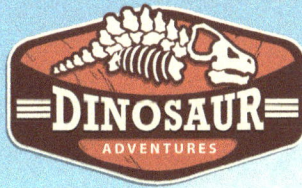

DINOSAUR
ADVENTURES

I0201569

Get to Know
Dinosaurs

공룡에
대해 알아보기

Alexis Roumanis

Explore other books at:
WWW.ENGAGEBOOKS.COM

VANCOUVER, B.C.

e WWW.ENGAGEBOOKS.COM

Get to Know Dinosaurs: Level 1 Bilingual (English/Korean) (영어/한국어)
Roumanis, Alexis 1982
Text © 2021 Engage Books

Edited by: Lauren Dick
Translated by: Gio Oh
Proofread by: Tamara Kazali

Text set in Arial Regular.
Chapter headings set in Arial Black.

FIRST EDITION / FIRST PRINTING

LIBRARY AND ARCHIVES CANADA CATALOGUING IN PUBLICATION

Title: Get to know dinosaurs Level 1 Bilingual (English/Korean) (영어/한국어)
Names: Roumanis, Alexis, author.
Description: Series statement: Dinosaur adventures

ISBN 978-1-77476-435-0 (hardcover)
ISBN 978-1-77476-434-3 (softcover)

Subjects:
LCSH: Readers
LCSH: Readers—Dinosaurs.

Classification: LCC PE1117 .D56 2021 | DDC J428.6—DC23

Contents
목차

What Are Dinosaurs?
공룡은 무엇인가요?

Dinosaurs are **reptiles**. The word dinosaur means "terrible lizard."
공룡은 파충류에요. 공룡은 끔찍한 도마뱀이라는 뜻이에요.

Reptiles are cold-blooded animals. They use heat from the Sun to stay warm.
파충류는 냉혈동물이에요. 그들은 따뜻하게 지내기위해 태양의 열을 이용해요.

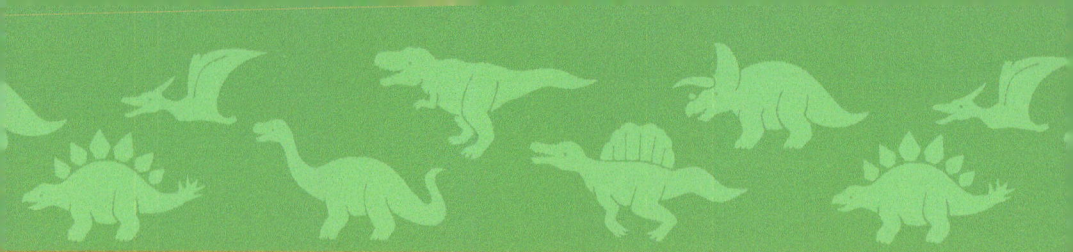

What Did Dinosaurs Look Like?
공룡은 어떻게 생겼었나요?

Dinosaurs walked on two or four legs. They all had tails. The smallest dinosaur was about the size of a chicken. The largest dinosaurs were bigger than some schools.

공룡은 두다리 또는 네개의 다리로 걸었어요. 모두 꼬리가 있었죠. 가장 작은 공룡은 크기가 닭만 했어요. 가장 큰 공룡은 몇몇 학교들보다 컸답니다.

> The nails on a Triceratops are called hooves. Some dinosaurs had claws.
> 트리케라톱스의 손톱은 발굽이라고 불러요. 몇몇 공룡은 발톱이 있었어요.

Horns and spikes helped to keep dinosaurs safe.
뿔과 가시는 공룡들을 안전하게 지켜줬어요.

Spikes
가시

Horns
뿔

Some dinosaurs had beaks just like birds.
몇몇 공룡들은 새처럼 부리가 있었어요.

When Did Dinosaurs Live?
공룡은 언제 살았나요?

Dinosaurs were the main animals on Earth for about 200 million years.

2억년전 지구에는 공룡이 지구의 주요 동물이었어요.

A large meteor hit Earth about 65 million years ago. Scientists think this is what killed most dinosaurs.
6천5백만년전 큰 운석이 지구를 강타했어요. 과학자들은 이 때문에 대부분 공룡이 죽었다고 생각해요.

9

Where Did Dinosaurs Live?
공룡은 어디에서 살았나요?

Earth looked very different when the dinosaurs lived. There was one large area of land called Pangea.

공룡들이 살던 지구는 지금과 매우 다릅니다. 판게아라고 부르는 큰 대륙 하나만 있었죠.

Over time, Pangea started to break apart. Tyrannosaurus Rex (T-Rex), Velociraptor, and Brachiosaurus lived in different areas on Pangea.
시간이 지나면서, 판게아는 여러개로 나눠지기 시작했어요. 티라노사우르스(티렉스), 벨로키랍토르와 브라키오사우루스는 판게아의 다른 지역에 살았어요.

Velociraptor
벨로키랍토르

T-Rex
티라노사우루스

Eurasia
유라시아

North America
북아메리카

Tethys Sea
테티스해

Brachiosaurus
브라키오사우루스

South America
남아메리카

Africa
아프리카

India
인도

Antarctica
남극

Australia
오스트레일리아

Panthalassic Ocean
판탈라사 해

2,000 miles
2,000 마일
0

4,000 kilometers
4,000 킬로미터
0

N

Legend 전설
☐ Land 육지
☐ Ocean 바다

What Did Dinosaurs Eat?
공룡은 무엇을 먹었나요?

Dinosaurs ate mostly meat or plants. Meat eating dinosaurs are called carnivores. Plant eating dinosaurs are herbivores.

공룡은 대부분 식물이나 고기를 먹었어요.
고기를 먹는 공룡은 육식동물이에요.
식물을 먹는 공룡은 초식동물이에요.

The Brachiosaurus' long neck
helped it to eat leaves on tall trees.
브라키오사우루스는 긴 목 덕분에 키가
큰 나무의 잎을 먹을 수 있었어요.

13

Dinosaur Life Cycle
공룡의 일생

All dinosaurs hatched from eggs.
모든 공룡은 알에서 부화했어요.

Baby dinosaurs are called hatchlings.
아기 공룡은 갓 부화류라고 불러요.

Young dinosaurs are called juveniles.
어린 공룡은 유아기에요.

T-Rex could live for about 30 years. But large plant-eating dinosaurs lived for about 80 years.
티렉스는 30년정도 살 수 있어요. 하지만 큰 초식동물은 80년 가까이 살 수 있었어요.

Curious Facts About Dinosaurs

Argentinosaurus weighed more than 17 elephants. It may be the largest land animal to have ever lived.
아르젠티노사우루스는 17마리의 코끼리를 다 합친 거보다 무거웠어요. 아마 지금까지 살았던 육지 동물들 중 가장 큰 동물일 수도 있어요.

Stegosaurus had a brain the size of a walnut.
스테고사우루스는 호두 정도 크기의 뇌를 가지고 있었어요.

Some dinosaurs had feathers.
몇몇 공룡은 깃털이 있었어요.

16

공룡에 대한 신기한 사실들

Most herbivores had spikes and horns to help protect themselves.
대부분의 초식동물은 스스로를 보호하기위해 가시나 뿔이 있었어요.

Pteranodon are not dinosaurs. They were flying reptiles that lived during the age of dinosaurs.
익룡은 공룡이 아니에요. 공룡이 살던 시대에 살았던 날아다니는 파충류였어요.

Humans have found more than 700 kinds of dinosaurs so far.
인간은 지금까지 700종이 넘는 공룡을 발견해 왔어요.

17

Kinds of Dinosaurs
공룡의 종류

Parasaurolophus had large head crests they used to make trumpeting sounds.
파라사우롤로푸스는 머리에 큰 볏을 가지고 있었고 트럼펫 소리를 내곤 했어요.

Dilophosaurus was one of the first large meat-eating dinosaurs.
딜로포사우루스는 최초의 거대한 육식공룡들 중 하나였어요.

Sauroposeidon was the tallest dinosaur. It was 59 feet (18 meters) tall.
사우로포세이돈은 가장 키가 큰 공룡이었어요. 높이가 59피트(18미터)였어요.

Tyrannosaurus Rex was about the size of a school bus.
티라노사우루스 렉스는 크기가 스쿨버스만 했어요.

Stegosaurus had spikes that helped protect it from carnivores.
스테고사우루스는 육식동물들로부터 보호할 수 있는 뾰족한 가시를 가지고 있었어요.

Velociraptor could run at speeds of about 40 miles (64 km) per hour.
벨로시랩터는 시속 약 40마일(64킬로미터)를 달릴 수 있었어요.

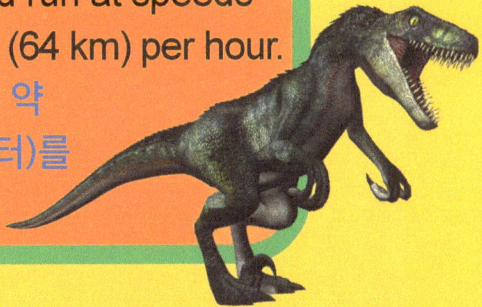

Spinosaurus was a good swimmer and ate fish.
스피노사우루스는 수영을 잘 했고 물고기를 잡아먹었어요.

What Is A Palaeontologist?
고생물학자는 무엇인가요?

Palaeontologists study plants and animals that lived millions of years ago.
고생물학자는 수백만년전에 살았던 식물과 동물을 연구합니다.

Palaeontologists study the remains of these living things. The remains are called fossils.

고생물학자는 이 생물들의 잔해를 연구합니다. 이 잔해는 화석이라고 불러요.

Finding Dinosaur Fossils
공룡 화석 찾기

Palaeontologists look for fossils all over the world. They use special tools to dig for fossils.

고생물학자는 전세계에서 화석을 찾으러 다녀요. 화석을 찾기위해 땅을 파는 특별한 도구를 사용한답니다.

Sometimes, palaeontologists will even find dinosaur footprints.
가끔, 고생물학자는 공룡의 발자국을 찾기도 해요.

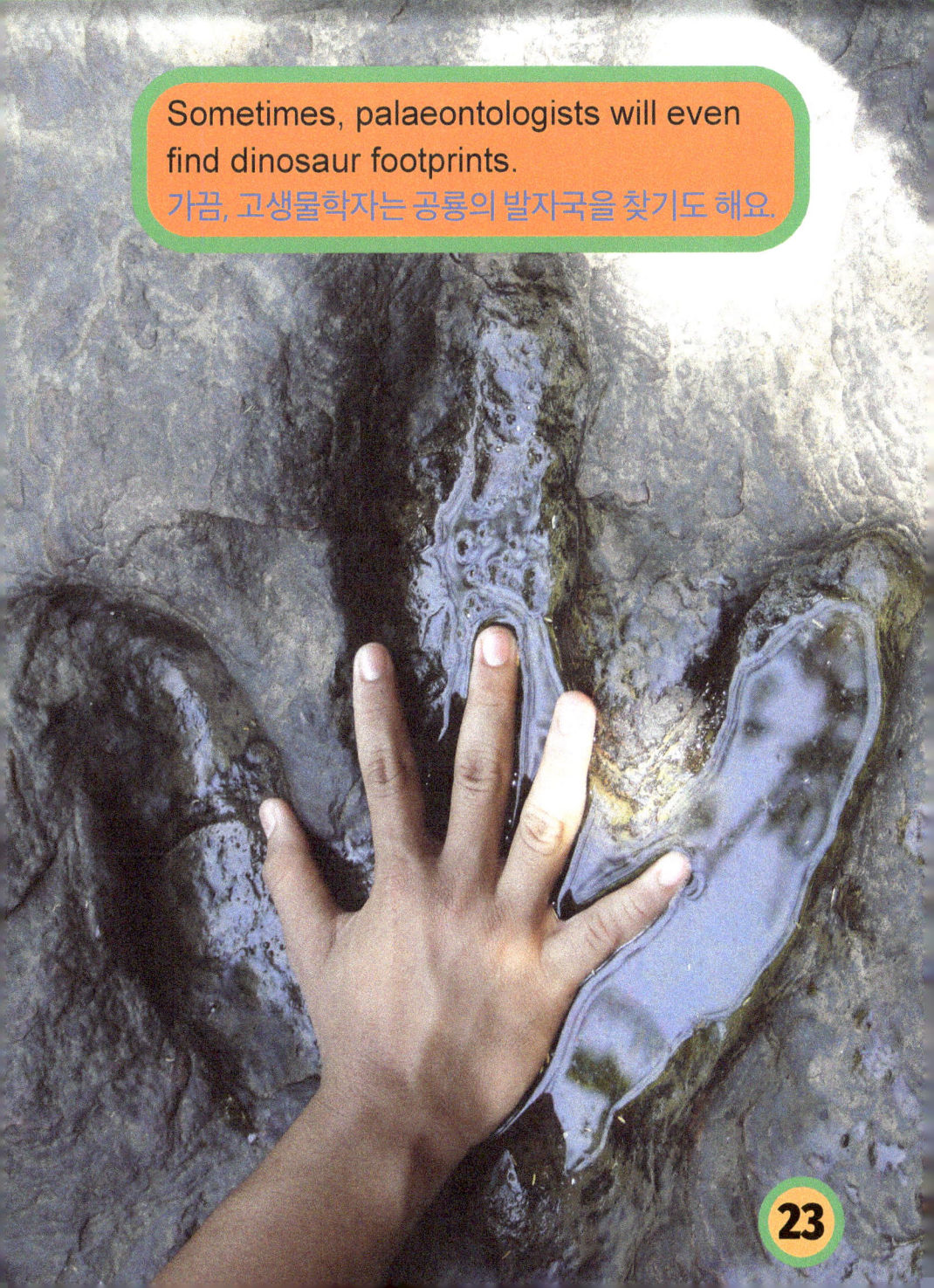

Dinosaur Museums
공룡 박물관

Some dinosaur fossils are pieced together like a puzzle. People can see them in a dinosaur museum.

몇몇 공룡 화석들은 퍼즐처럼 조각되어 있어요. 사람들은 공룡 박물관에서 이것들을 볼 수 있죠.

Seeing dinosaurs at a museum can be exciting. It is a great way to learn more about dinosaurs and how they lived.

박물관에서 공룡을 보는 것을 흥미로울 수 있어요. 이는 공룡들이 어디서 살았는지를 배울 수 있는 좋은 방법이에요.

Dinosaur Evolution
공룡의 진화

Over time, dinosaurs changed in shape and size. This is called evolution.
시간이 지나면서, 공룡의 모양과 크기가 변했어요. 이것은 진화라고 불리죠.

T-Rex evolved from a dinosaur that was the size of a human child.
티렉스는 인간 아이 크기의 공룡에서 진화했어요.

Protoceratops had no horns. It lived
2 million years before triceratops.
Protoceratops evolved into triceratops.
프로토케라톱스는 뿔이 없었어요.
트리케라톱스보다 2백만년 전에 살았었죠.
프로토케라톱스는 트리케라톱스로 진화했어요.

Protoceratops
프로토케라톱스

Triceratops had
three horns.
트리케라톱스는 세 개의
뿔을 가지고 있었어요.

How Dinosaurs Help Humans
공룡이 사람을 돕는 방법

Over time, Earth gets warmer and cooler. This is called climate change.
시간이 지나면서, 지구는 더 따뜻해지고 차가워졌어요. 이를 기후 변화라고 합니다.

Only ten thousand years ago, Earth was mostly covered in ice and snow.
불과 만 년 전만 해도 지구는 얼음과 눈으로 덮여 있었어요.

Paleontologists study how climate change affected dinosaurs. This helps them understand how climate change affects animals today.

고생물학자들은 기후변화가 공룡들에게 어떤 영향을 미쳤는지를 연구해요. 이는 오늘 날의 기후변화가 동물들에게 어떤 영향을 미치는지를 알 수 있게 해줘요.

Quiz
퀴즈

Test your knowledge of dinosaurs by answering the following questions. The questions are based on what you have read in this book. The answers are listed on the bottom of the next page.
아래 질문에 답하면서 공룡에 대한 지식을 테스트 해보세요. 질문은 책의 내용에 기반합니다. 정답은 다음 페이지 밑에 적혀 있어요.

1
What does the word dinosaur mean?
공룡의 뜻은 무엇인가요?

2
When did a large meteor hit Earth?
언제 큰 운석이 지구에 부딪혔나요?

3
What was Pangea?
판게아는 무엇인가요?

4
What are meat-eating dinosaurs called?
고기를 먹는 공룡은 뭐라고 부르나요?

5
What are baby dinosaurs called?
아기 공룡은 뭐라고 부르나요?

6
What remains do palaeontologists dig for?
고생물학자들은 무엇을 위해 땅을 파나요?

Explore Other Level 1 Bilingual English/Spanish Readers!

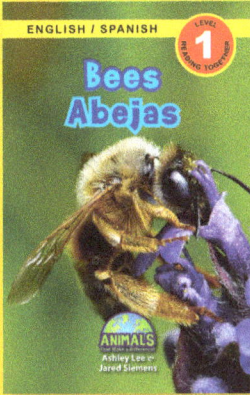

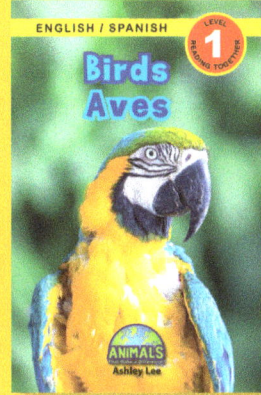

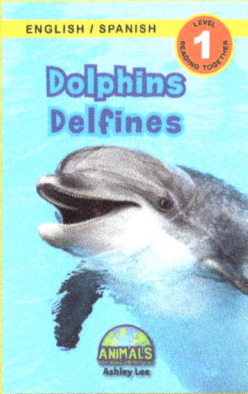

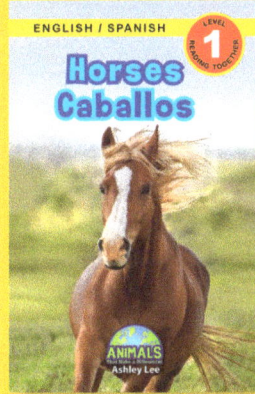

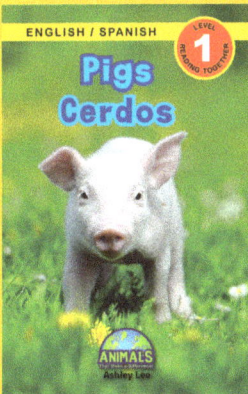

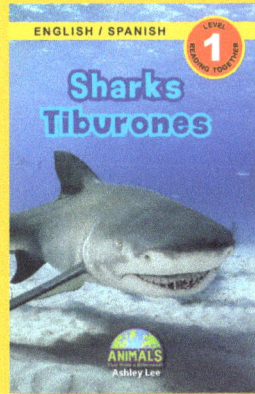

ENGLISH / SPANISH — LEVEL 1 READING TOGETHER
Bees
Abejas
ANIMALS That Make a Difference
Ashley Lee and Jared Siemens

ENGLISH / SPANISH — LEVEL 1 READING TOGETHER
Bats
Murciélagos
ANIMALS That Make a Difference
Ashley Lee

ENGLISH / SPANISH — LEVEL 1 READING TOGETHER
Birds
Aves
ANIMALS That Make a Difference
Ashley Lee

ENGLISH / SPANISH — LEVEL 1 READING TOGETHER
Dolphins
Delfines
ANIMALS That Make a Difference
Ashley Lee

ENGLISH / SPANISH — LEVEL 1 READING TOGETHER
Horses
Caballos
ANIMALS That Make a Difference
Ashley Lee

ENGLISH / SPANISH — LEVEL 1 READING TOGETHER
Ladybugs
Catarinas
ANIMALS That Make a Difference
Ashley Lee

ENGLISH / SPANISH — LEVEL 1 READING TOGETHER
Pigs
Cerdos
ANIMALS That Make a Difference
Ashley Lee

ENGLISH / SPANISH — LEVEL 1 READING TOGETHER
Sharks
Tiburones
ANIMALS That Make a Difference
Ashley Lee

ENGLISH / SPANISH — LEVEL 1 READING TOGETHER
Squirrels
Ardillas
ANIMALS That Make a Difference
Ashley Lee

Visit www.engagebooks.com to explore more Engaging Readers.

31

www.ingramcontent.com/pod-product-compliance
Lightning Source LLC
Chambersburg PA
CBHW051236020426
42331CB00016B/3401